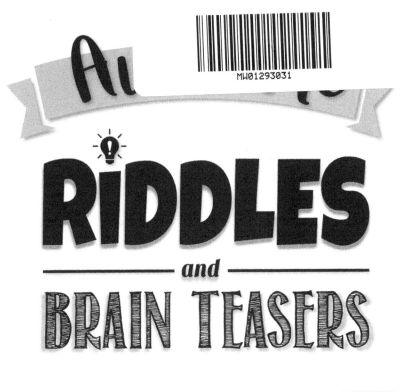

©2018 by Dan Gilden

All rights reserved.

No part of this publication may be reproduced, stored in a retrieval system, or transmitted, in any form or by any means, electronic, mechanical, photocopying, recording, or otherwise, without the prior permission of the copyright owner.

Dan Gilden

TABLE OF CONTENTS

Chapter One 3

Answers: #1-50 21

Chapter Two 26

Answers: #51-100 43

Chapter Three 49

Answers: #101-150 66

Chapter Four 72

Answers: #151-200 87

Chapter Five 92

Answers: #201-235 104

Your Review 108

CHAPTER One

Riddle #1

I've been around for millions of years, but I'm never more than a month old. What am I?

Riddle #2

I'm full of keys but I cannot open any door. What am I?

Riddle #3

It is weightless, you can see it, and if you put it in a barrel it will make the barrel lighter. What is it?

Riddle #4

I am a mother and a father but

have never given birth. I'm rarely still, but I never wander. What am I?

Riddle #5

I am a tasty fruit but you can also find me on a calendar. What am I?

Riddle #6

I C the C Above the C. What Do I C?

Riddle #7

It is an insect. Half of its name is another insect. What is it?

Riddle #8

When you have me, you immediately feel like sharing me. But, if you do share me, you do not have me. What am I?

Riddle #9

A necessity to some, a treasure to many, I'm best enjoyed in a pleasant company. Some like me cold, some like me hot. Some like me mild, some like me bold. What am I?

Riddle #10

It's in Arabic, but if you speak English, you probably use it every day. What is it?

Awesome Riddles

Riddle #11

I am a fruit. But if you take away the first letter from my name I become a crime. Take away the first two letters, I become an animal. Take away the first and last letter from my name and I become a type of music. What am I?

Riddle #12

Which is heavier: a pound of feathers or a pound of rocks?

Riddle #13

What never asks any questions but is always answered?

Riddle #14

What goes through a door but never goes in and never comes out?

Riddle #15

It is a word with two meanings. With one it can be broken, with the second it holds on. What is it?

Riddle #16

Who is bigger: Mr. Bigger, Mrs. Bigger, or their baby?

Riddle #17

Steve is turning 18 this year, yet

he turned 17 only yesterday. How is this possible?

Riddle #18

What runs around all day and then sits in the closet all night with its tongue hanging out?

Riddle #19

My eye is black, my mane is yellow. You can see me at the mart, and I can be taller than you, fellow. What am I?

Riddle #20

What can point in every direction but can't reach the destination by itself?

Riddle #21

When you don't know what I am, then I am something. But if you know what I am, then I am nothing. What am I?

Riddle #22

I can be thin but not fat. I'm in your body but never on your placemat. I'm always better when I'm fresh, but you'll never see me in the flesh. What am I?

Riddle #23

I have cities but no houses, oceans but without water, forests but no trees, deserts but no sand. What am I?

Riddle #24

One day a man left home and started to run. Then he turned left. Soon after, he turned left again. Then he started running home. When he returned home he saw two masked men. Who were they?

Riddle #25

The more you work, the more I'll eat. You keep me full, I'll keep you neat. What am I?

Riddle #26

He builds bridges of silver and crowns of gold. Who is he?

Riddle #27

What's always coming, but never arrives?

Riddle #28

What can be swallowed, but also can swallow you?

Riddle #29

I'm many people's favorite place, even though many do not remember their stay. You'll love to come and hate to leave, if you get cold you can use my sleeves. What am I?

Riddle #30

Which hand is best for stirring sugar into a cup of tea?

Riddle #31

A farmer has three fields. One of them has three bundles of hay, another has four, and the last one has five. How many would he have in the first field if he combined all of them in that field?

Riddle #32

I have one, and you have one. Remove part of it and you still have a bit. Remove another part, but bit is still remains. After much trying, you might be able to remove another part and it still remains. It dies hard! What is it?

Riddle #33

A man pushes his car, then stops in front of a hotel and immediately goes bankrupt. What is he doing?

Riddle #34

There are different kinds of it, but the one you pick doesn't do its job. What is it?

Riddle #35

I can fall down from the tallest

of buildings and survive, but drop me from the smallest ship and I won't. What am I?

Riddle #36

Six drinking glasses stand in a row. The first three are filled with juice and the last three are empty. By moving only one glass, can you arrange them so that the full and the empty glasses alternate?

Riddle #37

Name three consecutive days without using the words: Wednesday, Friday, or Sunday.

Riddle #38

I have keys but no locks. I have space but no room. You can enter but cannot go outside. What am I?

Riddle #39

Two fathers and two sons went ice skating one day. They all hired skates. But only three pairs of skates were hired. How is this possible?

Riddle #40

Why can't a man living in Ireland be buried in Scotland?

Riddle #41

People need it, but they always give it away. What is it?

Riddle #42

A man is trapped in a room. The room has only two doors. Through the first door, there is a room constructed from magnifying glass. The blazing hot sun instantly fries anyone who enters. Through the second door, there is a fire-breathing dragon. How does the man escape?

Riddle #43

What belongs to you but other

people use it more than you?

Riddle #44

What can be measured but not seen?

Riddle #45

I am a rare case where Today comes before Yesterday. What am I?

Riddle #46

Never resting, never still, silently moving from hill to hill. I do not walk, run or trot, but everything's cool where I am not. What am I?

Riddle #47

I have legs but not walk, a strong back but work not, two good arms but reach not, a seat but sit and tarry not. What am I?

Riddle #48

A taxi driver is going the wrong way down a one-way street. He passes three police officers, but none of them stops him. Why?

Riddle #49

What can you fill with empty hands?

Dan Gilden

Riddle #50

You can see nothing else, when you look in my face, I will look you in the eye, and I will never lie. What am I?

Awesome Riddles

ANSWERS #1-50

1) The moon.

2) A piano.

3) A hole.

4) A tree.

5) A date.

6) The crescent moon above the sea.

7) A beetle (Bee is the other insect)

8) A secret.

9) Coffee.

10) The Arabic numerals, 1, 2, 3,

etc.

11) Grape.

12) Neither. both weigh a pound!

13) A doorbell.

14) A keyhole.

15) Tie.

16) Their baby, because he is a "little bigger".

17) Steve's birthday is on December 31, the last day of the year. Today is January the 1st of the next year.

18) Your shoe.

19) A sunflower.

20) Your finger.

21) A riddle.

22) Air.

23) A map.

24) The umpire and the catcher. He was playing baseball.

25) Pencil sharpener.

26) A dentist.

27) Tomorrow.

28) The pride.

29) A bed.

30) It's better to use a spoon.

31) Just one, he combined them all.

32) A habit.

33) Playing Monopoly.

34) A lock.

35) A piece of paper.

36) Pour the juice from the 2nd glass into the 5th glass.

37) Yesterday, today, and tomorrow.

38) Keyboard.

39) They were a grandfather, a father, and the father's son.

40) Because he is alive.

41) Money.

42) He waits until nightfall and

then goes through the first door.

43) Your name.

44) Time.

45) A dictionary.

46) Sunlight (or sunshine).

47) A chair.

48) The taxi driver was on foot.

49) Gloves.

50) Reflection.

CHAPTER

Riddle #51

A cowboy rides into town on Monday. He stays for three days, then leaves on Monday. How is it possible?

Riddle #52

In a one-story red house, there was a red person, a red cat, a red dog, a red table, a red chair, and a red shower. What color were the stairs?

Riddle #53

Who can shave ten times a day and still have a beard?

Riddle #54

A window cleaner is cleaning a window on the 23rd floor when he slips and falls. He has no safety equipment and nothing to soften his fall, yet he is not hurt. How can this be?

Riddle #55

What grows only upwards and can never come down?

Riddle #56

I'm a family of seven: two are bitter and harsh, four are twins, the last is the warmest of all. What family am I?

Riddle #57

I'm red, blue, purple and green. No one can reach me, not even the queen. What am I?

Riddle #58

A little boy and a soldier are in the park. The boy is the soldier's son but the soldier is not the boy's father. How can this be?

Riddle #59

I go up and down the stairs without moving. Who Am I?

Riddle #60

A farmer has five chickens, two horses, and a wife. How many feet are on his farm?

Riddle #61

I can be long, I can be short. I can be grown, I can be bought. I can be painted or left bare. I can be round, or even square. What am I?

Riddle #62

If you put the coin in the bottle and a cork into the neck of the bottle, how can you get the coin out without breaking the bottle?

Riddle #63

No matter the shape I sit in, you will find me in a row. My name has no letters, but my initials are MNO. What am I?

Riddle #64

Large as a mountain, small as a pea, endlessly swimming in a waterless sea.

Riddle #65

You answer me, but I never ask you a question. What am I?

Riddle #66

A mirror for the famous, but

rmative to all. I'll show you the world, but it may be a bit small. What am I?

Riddle #67

How many colored pencils do I have if none are purple but all but three are green, all but three are pink, all but three are orange and all but three are blue?

Riddle #68

How many legs does a butterfly have if you call its antennae legs?

Riddle #69

It is an odd number. Take away one letter and it becomes even. What number is it?

Riddle #70

You can hold me in your hand and yet I can fill the entire room. What am I?

Riddle #71

Crawls over pages and fells wild beasts. Can guide you along in your home and on streets. What is it?

Riddle #72

I am taken from a mine, and shut up in a wooden case, from which I am never released, and yet I am used by everyone. What am I?

Riddle #73

You fill up a bathtub with water and you have a teaspoon, tablespoon, and a cup. What is the fastest way to empty the bathtub?

Riddle #74

You use me from your head to your toes, the more I work the thinner I grow. What am I?

Riddle #75

Jimmy's mother had four children. She named the first Monday. She named the second Tuesday, and she named the third Wednesday. What is the name of the fourth child?

Riddle #76

What are the next three letters in the following sequence: J, F, M, A, M, J, J, A, __, __, __?

Riddle #77

I am always overlooked by everybody but everybody has me. What am I?

Riddle #78

What three letters can change a boy into a man?

Riddle #79

What is as big as an elephant, but doesn't weigh anything?

Riddle #80

You may always chase me but you are always about three miles away. What am I?

Riddle #81

I have two arms, but fingers I have none. I've got two feet, but I cannot run. I carry well, but I carry best with my feet off the ground. What am I?

Riddle #82

Poke your fingers in my eyes and I will open wide my jaws. Quills, linen cloth, or paper, my hunger devours them all. What am I?

Riddle #83

It turns into a different story. What is it?

Riddle #84

What turns everything around but does not move?

Riddle #85

You can travel fast, but I travel faster. The faster you travel, the further away I get still. Close as you may get, the faster I still will be. What am I?

Riddle #86

I give advice to others, but I know nothing myself. I am a hitchhiker destined to stay still. What am I?

Riddle #87

I go up, I go down, towards the sky and the ground. I'm past and present tense too. Let's go for a ride, me and you. What am I?

Riddle #88

Give me food, and I will live. Give me water, and I will die. What am I?

Riddle #89

How can you stand behind your friend while he is standing behind you?

Riddle #90

What has arms but no hands and helps you see?

Riddle #91

I have 6 faces but not even one

body connected, 21 eyes in total but cannot see. What am I?

Riddle #92

I occur twice in eternity, and I'm always within sight. What am I?

Riddle #93

When I point up, it's bright. When I point down, it's dark. What am I?

Riddle #94

I have two backbones and thousands of ribs and I stretch across the land. What am I?

Riddle #95

A group of twelve people is going out for dinner but only two of them have an umbrella. Somehow they are able to walk all the way to the restaurant without getting wet. How?

Riddle #96

If the red house is on the left side and the blue house is on the right side where's the white house?

Riddle #97

I went into the woods and got it, I sat down to seek it, I brought it home with me because

I couldn't find it. What is it?

Riddle #98

What goes thousands of miles but never moves?

Riddle #99

What occurs once in a minute, twice in a moment, and never in a thousand years?

Riddle #100

It lives in winter, dies in spring, and grows with its roots on top. What is it?

ANSWERS #51-100

51) His horse's name was Monday.

52) There weren't any stairs; it was a one story house.

53) A barber.

54) He was cleaning the window from the inside.

55) Your height.

56) The Seven Seas. The first two are bitter and harsh, the north and south ones are the twins, and the Indian Ocean is the warmest of them all(Arctic Ocean, Antarctic Ocean, North Atlantic Ocean, South Atlantic Ocean, North Pacific

Ocean, South Pacific Ocean, Indian Ocean).

57) Rainbow.

58) The soldier in uniform is the boy's mother.

59) A carpet.

60) Just four. His wife has two feet, he has two feet, each chicken has two claws, each horse has four hooves.

61) Fingernail.

62) Push the cork into the bottle and shake out the coin.

63) The number 6 on a telephone keypad.

64) An asteroid.

65) A phone.

66) The television.

67) Four: one green, one pink, one orange, and one blue.

68) A butterfly has six legs. Calling its antennae legs doesn't make them legs.

69) Seven. When you take the "S" away you are left with "Even".

70) A light bulb.

71) An Arrow.

72) Pencil lead.

73) Just drain the water.

74) A bar of soap.

75) Jimmy. Because Jimmy's mother had four children.

76) S, O, N. The sequence is the first letters of the months of the year. (September, October, and November)

77) A nose.

78) Age.

79) A shadow of an elephant.

80) The horizon.

81) A wheelbarrow.

82) Scissors.

83) Spiral staircase.

Awesome Riddles

84) Mirror.

85) Light.

86) A road sign.

87) A seesaw.

88) Fire.

89) You both must be standing back to back.

90) A pair of glasses.

91) A dice.

92) The letter 't'.

93) A light switch.

94) Train tracks.

95) It's not raining.

96) In Washington DC.

97) A splinter.

98) Highway.

99) The letter "M".

100) An icicle.

Awesome Riddles

CHAPTER
Three

Riddle #101

What do you throw out when you want to use it and take it in when you don't want to use it?

Riddle #102

What can be quick and deadly and gathers by the ocean?

Riddle #103

Here is the Roman numeral for nine: IX. By adding only one line or symbol, how can you turn it into 6?

Riddle #104

I am worthless, yet when added

to others I add worth. What am I?

Riddle #105

What gets whiter the dirtier it gets?

Riddle #106

There are 12 months in a year. Seven months have 31 days. How many months have 28 days?

Riddle #107

What kind of room has no doors or windows?

Riddle #108

Different lights make me

strange, for each one my size will change. What am I?

Riddle #109

What is a word made up of 4 letters, yet is also made up of 3? Sometimes is written with 9 letters, and then with 4. Rarely consists of 6, and never is written with 5.

Riddle #110

I join you in battle, fist clenched tight. We pound three times with all our might. If my rival decides he will sign for peace; I'll crush him, and the fight will cease. But if he lays his hand down flat; I'll suffer defeat, that is that. What am I?

Riddle #111

How many seconds are there in one year?

Riddle #112

It brings light to a dark world. In a current it travels and through tunnels it's hurled. Touch it and it will kill you. What is it?

Riddle #113

If the day after tomorrow is yesterday, today will be as far from Wednesday as today was from Wednesday when the day before yesterday was tomorrow. What is tomorrow?

Riddle #114

Alive without breath, as cold as death; Never thirsty, ever drinking, all in mail never clinking. What is it?

Riddle #115

What is so delicate that uttering one word will break it?

Riddle #116

What was the tallest mountain in the world, before Mount Everest was discovered?

Riddle #117

I turn around once, what is outside will not get in. I turn around again, what is inside will not get out. What am I?

Riddle #118

Imagine that you are in a boat, in the middle of the sea. Suddenly, you are surrounded by hungry sharks, just waiting to feed on you. How can you put an end to this?

Riddle #119

How many bricks does it take to finish a building?

Riddle #120

If you have three, you have three. If you have two, you have two. But if you have one, you have none. What is it?

Riddle #121

What 9-letter word still remains a word each time you remove one letter from it?

Riddle #122

What Is always in front of you but cannot be seen?

Riddle #123

What body part is pronounced as

one letter but written with three. Only two different letters are used?

Riddle #124

Tom Smith was born on January 25th, yet her birthday is always in the summer. How is this possible?

Riddle #125

What goes around the world but always stays in a corner?

Riddle #126

What ancient invention lets you look right through a wall?

Riddle #127

You throw away the outside and cook the inside, then you eat the outside and throw away the inside. What is it?

Riddle #128

I exist only when there is light, but direct light kills me. What am I?

Riddle #129

How can a man go 8 days without sleep?

Riddle #130

This old one runs forever, but

never moves at all. He has not lungs nor throat, but still a mighty roaring call. What is it?

Riddle #131

Take off my skin — I won't cry, but you will! What am I?

Riddle #132

What gets bigger every time you take away from it?

Riddle #133

What flies when it's born, lies when it's alive, and runs when it's dead?

Riddle #134

The 22nd and 24th presidents of the USA had the same parents but were not brothers. How is this possible?

Riddle #135

You eat something you neither plant nor plow. It comes from water, but if water touches it, it dies. What is it?

Riddle #136

What breaks on the water but never on land?

Riddle #137

What 4-letter word can be written forward, backward and upside down, but can still be read from left to right?

Riddle #138

I'm flat when I'm new. I'm fat when you use me. I release my gas when something sharp touches me. What am I?

Riddle #139

A family lives on a 10th floor in an apartment building. Every day their son takes the elevator from the 10th floor to the ground floor and goes to school. When he returns home, he uses the elevator to get to the fifth floor, and then uses the stairs for the remaining 5 floors. Why?

Riddle #140

A man is sitting in his cabin in Michigan. 3 hours later he gets out of his cabin in Dallas. How is this possible?

Riddle #141

If you look at my face there won't be 13 any place. What am I?

Riddle #142

You wear me all the time but you never put me on. I will change colors if you leave me out too long. What am I?

Riddle #143

A man was driving a black car. His lights were off. The moon shown no light. A black cat was in the middle of the road. How did he know when to stop?

Riddle #144

Which one is correct? "Penguins flies" or "A Penguin flies".

Dan Gilden

Riddle #145

Countless blades that bend with a touch, exploited by kids who want to make a buck. What am I?

Riddle #146

I am a ship that can be made to ride the greatest waves. I am not built by tools but built by hearts and minds. What am I?

Riddle #147

Sometimes I'm high and sometimes low. I creep between your toes. My orders come right from the sky, I make men fall and rise. What am I?

Riddle #148

What is two days after the day after the day before yesterday?

Riddle #149

You twirl my body but I keep my head up high. When I go in I keep things tight. What am I?

Riddle #150

20 pigeons sat on the branches of a tree. A man shot 1 pigeon with his gun. How many were left on the tree?

ANSWERS #101-150

101) An anchor.

102) Sand.

103) SIX.

104) 0 (Zero). Zero is nothing, but when you add zeroes to a number like 1, it becomes 10, 100 or 1,000.

105) A chalkboard.

106) They all do.

107) A mushroom.

108) The pupil.

109) Correct, the word 'what' has 4 letters in it, 'yet' has 3,

'sometimes' has 9, 'then' has 4, 'rarely' has 6, and 'never' has 5.

110) The rock in rock-paper-scissors.

111) Only 12. January 2nd, February 2nd, etc.

112) Electricity.

113) Thursday.

114) Fish.

115) Silence.

116) Mount Everest. Just because it wasn't discovered didn't make it smaller.

117) A Key.

118) Stop imagining!

119) One (the last one is the only one that can finish the building).

120) Choices.

121) Startling, starting, staring, string, sting, sing, sin, in, I.

122) The future.

123) Eye.

124) He lives in the Southern Hemisphere.

125) A stamp.

126) The window.

127) Corn on the cob because you throw away the husk, cook and eat the kernels, and throw away the cob.

Awesome Riddles

128) Shadow.

129) He sleeps at night.

130) A Waterfall.

131) Onion.

132) A hole.

133) Snowflake.

134) It was the same man. Grover Cleveland is the only president in the history of USA who served two, non-consecutive terms.

135) Salt.

136) A wave.

137) Noon.

138) Balloon.

139) Because he cannot reach the buttons higher than five.

140) He is a pilot in the cabin of the airplane.

141) A Clock.

142) Skin.

143) It was a bright sunny day.

144) Neither. Penguins don't fly.

145) Grass.

146) Friendship.

147) The tide.

148) Tomorrow. The day before yesterday is two days ago. The day after the day before yesterday (2 days ago) is yesterday. And two

days after yesterday is tomorrow.

149) A screw.

150) None. The rest flew away.

CHAPTER
Four

Riddle #151

I sleep by day, I fly by night. I have no feathers to aid my flight. What am I?

Riddle #152

I touch your hair, I'm in your words, I'm lack of space and loved by birds.

Riddle #153

A man is in his car. He sees three doors: a diamond-studded door, a gold door, and a silver door. Which door does he open first?

Riddle #154

I'm rarely touched but often held and if you're wise you'll use me well. What am I?

Riddle #155

Whats 3/7 chicken, 2/3 cat, and 2/4 goat?

Riddle #156

Which letter of the English alphabet flies, sings, and stings?

Riddle #157

There's a place on Earth where the wind blows south then suddenly north. Where is it?

Riddle #158

I take whatever you receive and surrender it all by waving my flag. What am I?

Riddle #159

I do not have any special powers, but I can predict the score of any football game before it begins. How can I do this?

Riddle #160

I'm the part of a bird that is not in the sky. I can swim in the sea and remain dry. What am I?

Riddle #161

What's nowhere but everywhere except where something is?

Riddle #162

You draw a line. Without touching it, how do you make the line longer?

Riddle #163

What sleeps through the day and cries through the night. The more it cries, the more it produces light?

Riddle #164

What gets sharper the more you

use it?

Riddle #165

What five-letter word becomes shorter when you add two letters to it?

Riddle #166

You go at red but stop at green. What am I?

Riddle #167

Big as a biscuit, deep as a cup, even a river can't fill it up. What is it?

Riddle #168

A word I know, six letters it

contains. Remove just one, and twelve remains. What am I?

Riddle #169

I'm made for one but meant for two; I can be worn for many years but sometimes just a few. You won't ever need me unless you say you do. What am I?

Riddle #170

If there are 6 apples and you take away 4, how many do you have?

Riddle #171

I drape the hills in white. I do

not swallow, but I sure do bite. What am I?

Riddle #172

What has many branches but no leaves?

Riddle #173

What is black and white and read all over?

Riddle #174

Who rows quickly with four oars but never comes out from under his own roof?

Riddle #175

People buy me to eat, but never

eat me. What am I?

Riddle #176

What has no beginning, end or middle?

Riddle #177

A boy fell off a 100-foot ladder but did not get hurt. Why not?

Riddle #178

No matter how much rain comes down on it, it won't get any wetter. What is it?

Riddle #179

We are measured in temperature and time but have neither. What are we?

Riddle #180

What is bought by the yard but worn by the foot?

Riddle #181

At night they come without being fetched, and by day they are lost without being stolen. What are they?

Riddle #182

The more you have of it, the less you see. What is it?

Riddle #183

Mr. Johnson has four daughters.

Each of his daughters has a brother. How many children does Mr. Johnson have?

Riddle #184

You can easily touch me, but not see me. You can throw me out, but not away. What am I?

Riddle #185

What has one foot but not a single leg?

Riddle #186

What has 10 letters and starts with gas?

Riddle #187

What two words, when combined hold the most letters?

Riddle #188

It is something that we always return but we never borrow. What is it?

Riddle #189

You are in a cabin and it is pitch black. You only have one match. Which do you light first, the newspaper, the lamp, the candle, or the fire?

Riddle #190

What starts with 't' and ends with 't' and only has 't' inside?

Riddle #191

The more you take, the more you leave behind. What are they?

Riddle #192

What kind of coat is best put on wet?

Riddle #193

I have an eye but am blind; a sea, but no water; a bee, but no honey; tea but no coffee; and a why, but no answer. What am I?

Riddle #194

You can eat me late at night, but never in the morning. What am I?

Riddle #195

What can split itself before splitting something else?

Riddle #196

If you are running in a race and you pass the person in second place, what place are you in?

Riddle #197

What verb becomes its own past tense by rearranging its letters?

Riddle #198

What has one eye but cannot see?

Riddle #199

You are my brother, but I am not your brother. Who am I?

Riddle #200

Four legs up, four legs down, soft in the middle, hard all around.

ANSWERS #151-200

151) A bat.

152) Air.

153) His car door.

154) Your tongue.

155) Chicago.

156) 'B' (BEE).

157) The South Pole. Until it reaches the pole it is going south, then as it passes the pole it is going north.

158) A mailbox.

159) The score before any game is always zero to zero!

160) A bird's shadow.

161) Nothing.

162) You draw a shorter line next to it.

163) A candle.

164) Your brain.

165) Short.

166) Watermelon.

167) A kitchen strainer.

168) Dozens.

169) Wedding ring.

170) The four apples you took!

171) Frost.

172) A Bank.

173) Newspaper.

174) Turtle.

175) Plate.

176) A donut.

177) He fell off the bottom step.

178) Water.

179) Longitude and latitude.

180) Carpet.

181) Stars.

182) Darkness.

183) He has five children, all of the daughters have the same brother.

184) Your back.

185) A snail.

186) Automobile.

187) Post office.

188) Thanks.

189) You light the match first!

190) A teapot.

191) Footprints.

192) A coat of paint.

193) Alphabet.

194) Dinner!

195) Lightning.

196) Second place.

197) Eat (ate).

198) Needle.

Awesome Riddles

199) I am your sister.

200) Bed.

Dan Gilden

CHAPTER
Five

Riddle #201

I jump when I walk and sit when I stand. What am I?

Riddle #202

What is easy to get into, but hard to get out of?

Riddle #203

I'm lighter than a feather, yet the strongest man can't hold me for more than 5 minutes. What am I?

Riddle #204

If you take away the whole, some still remains. What is it?

Riddle #205

If an electric train is going east at 60 miles an hour and there is a strong westerly wind, which way does the smoke from the train drift?

Riddle #206

I open to close and I close to open. I'm surrounded by water, but I'm never soaking. What am I?

Riddle #207

There are two planes. One is going from New York to Los Angeles at a speed of 500 MPH. The other is going from Los

Angeles to New York at a speed of 400 MPH. When the planes meet which one will be closer to Los Angeles?

Riddle #208

Which letter of the alphabet contains a lot of water?

Riddle #209

You hear it speak, for it has a hard tongue. But it cannot breathe, for it has not a lung. What is it?

Riddle #210

What is the easiest way to double your cash?

Riddle #211

What breaks and never falls and what falls and never breaks?

Riddle #212

What can run but never walks, has a mouth but never talks, has a head but never weeps, has a bed but never sleeps?

Riddle #213

I can't speak but I know a lot. I'm not a tree but I have leaves. I have hinges but I am neither a window nor a door. What am I?

Awesome Riddles

Riddle #214

What rock group consists of four famous members but none of them sings?

Riddle #215

There are several books on a bookshelf. One of the books is the 4th from the left and 6th from the right. How many books are on the shelf?

Riddle #216

If you have 30 black socks, 22 white socks, and 14 red socks scattered across the floor in the dark room, how many would you have to grab to get a matching pair?

Riddle #217

What is the best way to poke a balloon without popping it?

Riddle #218

How can you throw a ball as hard as you can, to only have it come back to you, even if it doesn't bounce off anything?

Riddle #219

What is the only question you can never answer yes to?

Riddle #220

What word is spelled wrong in

every dictionary?

Riddle #221

What has hands but no feet, a face but no eyes, tells but doesn't talk?

Riddle #222

What is full of holes but can still hold water?

Riddle #223

Poor people have it, rich people need it. And if you eat it, you die. What is it?

Riddle #224

You're a bus driver. At the first

stop, 5 people get on. At the second stop, 6 people get on. At the third stop 3 people get off and, at the fourth stop everyone got off. What color are the bus driver's eyes?

Riddle #225

What has a neck but no head?

Riddle #226

A man is twenty years old but has only had five birthdays. How is that possible?

Riddle #227

I can't go left I can't go right. I am stuck in a building over three stories high. What am I?

Riddle #228

I'm tall when I'm young; I'm short when I'm old. What am I?

Riddle #229

If it took eight men ten hours to build a wall, how long would it take four men to build it?

Riddle #230

What has a head and a tail but no body?

Riddle #231

You will always find me in the past. I can be created in the present, but the future can never taint me. What am I?

Riddle #232

I am a box that holds keys without locks, yet they can unlock your soul. What am I?

Riddle #233

A box without hinges, lock or key, yet golden treasure lies within. What is it?

Riddle #234

What tastes better than it smells?

Awesome Riddles

Riddle #235

How do you make the number one disappear?

ANSWERS #200-235

201) A kangaroo.

202) Trouble.

203) Breath.

204) Wholesome.

205) There is no smoke coming from electric trains.

206) A drawbridge.

207) They will be the same distance away when they meet.

208) The C.

209) Bell.

210) Put it in front of the mirror!

211) Day breaks, night falls.

212) River.

213) A book.

214) The faces on the Mount Rushmore.

215) Nine.

216) Four. Once you grab four you will definitely have two of the same color.

217) Do it when it's not blown up!

218) Throw the ball straight up in the air.

219) Are you asleep yet?

220) Wrong.

221) A clock.

222) A sponge.

223) Nothing.

224) The same as yours. You're the bus driver.

225) A bottle.

226) He was born on Leap Year Day. (The leap day is an extra day we add to the shortest month of the year, February. A leap year comes once every four years.)

227) Elevator.

228) Candle.

229) No time at all. It is already built.

230) A coin.

231) History.

232) Piano.

233) Egg.

234) Tongue.

235) Add the letter G. Now it's G-ONE!

THE END!

Dan Gilden

PLEASE LEAVE A REVIEW

I hope your kids have enjoyed reading this book. And it would be great if you could take a moment of your time to write down a short review on the book's Amazon Page. Your feedback is important to me. It will also help others to make an informed decision before purchasing this book.

THANK YOU!

Made in the USA
Middletown, DE
03 December 2019